ABC Z...
GU...
CLAMS UP

I CAN READ LEVEL 3

Written by Stefanie Hohl
Illustrated by Jennifer Bartlett

Playful Learning Press

www.abcseeheardo.com

ISBN 978-1-63824-028-0

Note to Parents, Caregivers, and Teachers:

The ABC Zoo Kids series builds on literacy skills introduced in the ABC See, Hear, Do Learn-to-Read series. Once children master the letter sounds in Level Three, they are ready to read a real story! Corresponding animal illustrations from *ABC See, Hear, Do Level Three: Learn to Read Blended Beginning Sounds* are included throughout the text of the story.

Our goal is to provide a complete story that children can read all on their own! Traditional early reader books often include difficult words that children struggle to sound out, which can make reading frustrating. This book contains only CVC & CCVC words, just like those your child practiced reading in ABC See, Hear, Do Levels 1 & 2, and *ABC See, Hear, Do Level Three: Learn to Read Blended Beginning Sounds*.

Tips for using this book:

- Allow children to read freely, using clues as a guide.

- If children are stuck on a letter or letter blend, remind them of the hand motion and corresponding sound.

- If children are stuck on a word, model reading the word by dragging your finger under each letter and demonstrating how to blend the letter sounds together.

- Once children are confident, try covering the animal clues with your hand or a sheet of paper.

- Every few pages, pause and talk about the story. Ask children questions to make sure they are comprehending what they are reading.

- If children are only "reading" the illustrations, try covering an illustration until they read the words below. Ask them what they predict will be included in the illustration to gauge whether they are understanding what they are reading. Then show them the picture!

Above all, remember that children learn at their own pace, and there's no need to rush. Remember, the goal here is to build confidence that will propel children throughout their literacy journey. So have fun together!

Pronunciation of words is based on General American English, or Broadcast English.

YAK

PORCUPINE

RACCOON

FLAMINGO

HIPPO

ELEPHANT

LION

ANT

NARWHAL

WALRUS

OCTOPUS

TURTLE

SALAMANDER

X-RAY TETRA FISH

VULTURE

KANGAROO

QUAIL

IGUANA

Gus and Viv skip.

"Fran!"

Fran and Viv chat.

Gus clams up.

Gus frets.

Gus zigs and zags.

Gus runs.

"Oz?"

Oz clams up.

Oz frets.

Oz zigs and zags.

Oz swims.

Gus scans.

Gus spots Oz.

"Crab?" Gus prods.

Oz grins. Gus grins.

Oz snags it.

Fran and Viv skip.

Oz spins.

Fran and Viv clap.

"Gum?"

"Yum."

"Gum?" Fran prods.

"Yes!" Gus grins.

Gus snags it.

"Yum, yum, yum!"

Oz spins and spins.

Viv, Fran, and
Gus spin and spin.

Viv, Fran, Gus, and Oz grin.

Made in the USA
Middletown, DE
12 August 2024

58950285R00020